What Can I Do?

An Alphabet for Living

LISA HARROW

Introduction by Roger Payne

CHELSEA GREEN PUBLISHING COMPANY
WHITE RIVER JUNCTION, VERMONT

Copyright © 2004 by Lisa Harrow
Introduction copyright © 2004 by Roger Payne

Managing Editor: Collette Leonard
Project Editor: Marcy Brant
Intern: Sue DuBois
Proofreader: Rachael Cohen
Designer: Peter Holm, Sterling Hill Productions
Design Assistant: Daria Hoak, Sterling Hill Productions

Printed in Canada
First printing, August, 2004

10 9 8 7 6 5 4 3 2 1

Printed on acid-free, recycled paper

Library of Congress Cataloging-in-Publication Data
Harrow, Lisa.
    What can I do? : an alphabet for living / Lisa Harrow ; introduction by Roger
Payne.
        p. cm.
    ISBN 1-931498-66-0 (pbk.)
    1. Nature—Effect of human beings on. 2. Environmental degradation. 3.
Environmental policy. 4. Environmental responsibility. I. Title.
    GF75.H37 2004
    333.72—dc22

                            2004016720

Chelsea Green Publishing Company
Post Office Box 428
White River Junction, VT 05001
(800) 639-4099
www.chelseagreen.com

For my father,
Ken Harrow,
who planted the seed

⁂

For my husband,
Roger Payne,
who nurtured its growth

⁂

For my son,
Tim Harrow,
who will reap the harvest

~~ ACKNOWLEDGMENTS ~~

My thanks to:

Pam and Peter Logan, whose interest and help made the first edition possible

Edith Crocker for designing the first edition and for her friendshop

Liz Ambros, without whom neither my life nor my computer would work

Maria Coughlin and John Crockett for early research

Doug Harmsen for his informed comments

Margo Baldwin for her vision and encouragement

Marcy Brant for being a wonderfully patient editor

Roger Payne for providing a bureau of standards, and love

Lisa Harrow

May 25, 1991, was a beautiful day in London, with an uncharacteristically clear blue sky. Looking back, my eight-year-old son Tim and I, if we were at all superstitious, might have taken such a beautiful day as a sign that our lives were about to change. Forever. But that kind of prescience only happens in fairy stories. The reality of our day was that we were heading to a "Save the Whales" rally in Trafalgar Square—something we'd never done before. Greenpeace had asked me to be a "celebrity speaker," to read a piece about how some whales communicate across thousands of miles of deep ocean with sounds that can also travel through the mantle of the Earth. That astonished me. Even though I had grown up in New Zealand where whales were once abundant, I knew nothing about these mysterious animals. The only whale I'd ever seen had been lying dead on the beach.

We stood at the back of a large crowd and watched the opening speech delivered by one Roger Payne, heralded for his work on whale song. That too was a surprise to me. I'd never heard of such a thing. He was an impassioned speaker, but I was much more focused on my nerves than on what he was saying. This was the first time I had ever addressed a large crowd without the carapace of a play, a character, and weeks of rehearsal to protect me.

Roger was at the foot of the stairs when I finished my piece. "Have you ever seen a whale from close quarters?" The voice was warm and humorous, matching the eyes. I said I hadn't, and as we talked, we began making plans to do so in the summer, and I found myself thinking of all the adventures we could share with this extraordinarily charming man who was so full of amazing stories. My complex life as a working actress and a single mother suddenly seemed so simple in comparison. Three hours later we were still talking. Ten weeks later we were married.

Meeting Roger was transformational. Standing there exchanging words and ideas with him, enfolding large chunks of our lives into passionate abbreviations—as one does upon instantly falling in love with someone—I felt as if I were at the edge of an ocean, ankle-deep in the incoming waves, staring out at the vast expanse of sunlit possibilities.

We were married in Woodstock, Vermont, that summer and the adventures began. Tim and I started spending time with whales and experiencing their awesome size and sheer beauty. Off the coast of California we watched dolphins riding on the bow waves of incomprehensibly huge blue whales. At Peninsula Valdez in Argentina we were lulled to sleep by the sound of right whales breathing in the bay. In Alaska we heard the piercing cries of humpbacks right through our boat as they corralled fish in their nets made from bubbles, and we watched amazed as they erupted out of the depths, mouths gaping wide to engulf the fish. Sitting in a small open boat in Laguna San Ignacio we stroked the head of a grey whale that came alongside for a visit. With the adventures came a growing understanding of Roger's world, and through that understanding, a gradual awakening to the environmental problems Earth faces.

We learned that everything in nature is connected. Human beings are not separate from the rest of life on Earth but an integral part of it. Thus everything we do has consequences: seemingly pristine lakes in the far north have fish that are heavily polluted with industrial chemicals produced thousands of miles away, deposited there by circulating air currents. The relentless development of new ways to harvest more and more fish from the ocean is resulting in fewer and fewer fish to catch. The worthy pursuit of cheap food is destroying soils and wildlife, and filling our bodies with toxins that disrupt hormones and diminish the ability of our children to learn. Access to fresh water is becoming a serious problem worldwide.

Two years ago, Roger conceived the idea of *Lessons from Copernicus*, a performance involving us both, which uses science and poetry to highlight both the problems and the exciting solutions that humanity is inventing to solve those problems. After our first performance I saw that many of the audience were overwhelmed by the enormity of the environmental stresses we face. It was clear they wanted to do something but didn't know where to start. I realized we needed to give them a tool to help them gain a deeper understanding of what is going wrong, and what they can do to become part of the solution. So I put together a small book full of useful Internet sites, to be given away free to everyone who came to the performance.

That first little book very quickly grew into this one and I hope it finds a home by your computer as a useful guide into the future. I think the Internet is one of humanity's greatest inventions. It allows us access to the information we need to make good decisions about how we live. It empowers us, it joins us together in common causes, and together we can have more effect in fighting for those causes than many Washington lobbyists, who seldom represent our best interests.

For years I had gone about my life aware somewhere on the periphery of my concerns that fish were becoming a scarce resource, that the rainforests were being destroyed, that modern agricultural and industrial practices were debilitating our world and us, but not really paying much attention. Life with Roger changed my focus. I began to think about the consequences of each action. I began to change the way I lived. I recycled. I filled our house with energy-efficient machines and compact fluorescent bulbs. I bought a hybrid car. I became aware of what we were eating and how it arrived on our plates. I became passionate about the possibility of transforming lakes of manure into electricity, thus solving the awful problems of groundwater pollution and appalling smell created by such manure lagoons. I began to carry around lists of which fish are healthy to eat and to share those lists with my friends and the waiters in restaurants. I started noticing wind farms wherever I was in the world, marveling at their silent beauty and at all the clean electricity they are producing. I started buying plastic bags made from corn. And most of all, I began to get very assertive about not wasting water.

Changing the way we live requires that we first understand what the problems are, their causes, and how to solve them. This book will introduce you to simple but revolutionary choices that can profoundly affect your health and the health of the rest of life on Earth. If we follow the laws of nature when producing energy, dealing with wastes, growing food, and manufacturing things, the destruction will stop. Life on Earth will continue into an unimagined future where, generations hence, our children's children will bless us and thank us for our heedfulness. And we can be proud that we are part of the twenty-first century revolution, where ordinary people are dreaming of, demanding, and achieving solutions beyond anything previously thought possible.

"Never doubt that a small group of thoughtful, committed citizens can change the world. Indeed, it is the only thing that ever has."

—Margaret Meade

Roger Payne

When I met Lisa Harrow at that Greenpeace rally, I fell in love with her in the first forty-five seconds, maybe less. When she was speaking I couldn't see her from where I was standing, but the intelligence of her voice came burning through all the traffic and hubbub of Trafalgar Square. As he thanked Lisa, the host of the rally said, "I wish all of you could see Miss Harrow's blue eyes up close. She has such beautiful eyes." He was dead right. But I think it was her fierce intelligence that stole my heart so entirely. As we talked I quickly established that neither of us was married or involved with anyone else, and all I could think of was, "How can I marry this extraordinary creature?"

I was staying with a friend in London who knew Lisa's work from television, and that night when I told him about having met her, and that I was determined to marry her, he turned to his partner, and murmured, "In his dreams."

At the moment I met Lisa, Tim was off with his nanny, playing on Trafalgar Square's famous bronze lions. By the time he appeared, half an hour later, I had realized that although Lisa and I could probably always get along, unless Tim approved, it would never work. So from the moment I met him I was determined that Tim should never feel left out of anything we did. Thus, our first date, which was the following morning, became a trip to the London zoo with Lisa, Tim, his nanny, and two cousins. Two weeks later, although we had hardly seen each other, Lisa had agreed to marry me.

But I felt that I must ask Tim for her hand, and that if he didn't approve we shouldn't go through with it. It was the scariest phone call I've ever made. But when I'd screwed up my courage and blurted out my request, he calmly said, "Yes," and then, with a dignity that only an extraordinary eight-year-old can achieve he said, "This is the happiest day of my life." Heaven knows, it was mine.

Because I could work from anywhere with a phone and a laptop computer, I moved to London after we were married and started accompanying Lisa wherever her work took her. When she did a play I tried to see all the performances (I watched her do *Wit* forty-two times), and from this I began to appreciate more fully her extraordinary ability. I saw that she could speak not just to someone's reason, but to their soul, and I realized that if it were possible to focus the burning glass of that ability on the problems humanity is creating for the environment, she might start bigger waves propagating through the human psyche than any mere scientist could ever achieve. It is with that in mind that I set out to write *Lessons from Copernicus*—a program we could do together.

Its message would be about the importance of our species living in accordance with the laws of nature—by doing everything sustainably. One of the most appealing reasons for embracing such a major lifestyle change would be the sheer delight of the vistas that would open up to people everywhere as each of us made our way along the road to sustainability—and learned to live in the world without destroying it. It would transform our current landscape of despair into one of hope.

As Lisa and I researched our program, an exciting, unexpected, and hopeful reality appeared: that humanity's worst problems are *solvable*; that most solutions are *simple*; and that existing scientific knowledge is *sufficient*.

It is clear that current science provides enough understanding to act; it is our collective will that needs work. And what could Lisa and I do to help fortify that will? Such fortification has occurred before when dissatisfaction with the status quo has roused people to action, and the success of their actions has energized their wills enough to trigger true change. It always seems to have been a process involving both information and inspiration. Perhaps Lisa and I could engage listeners by combining the inspiration of art and poetry with the information of science—thereby approaching their minds through both sides of their brains.

We had started from a sense of hopelessness, but our first effort at this dual approach convinced us that it might just have value. In any case, we could see that it lay on a path toward hope, where small nudges can unleash cascades of beneficial change. It seemed obvious that millions of people await a movement they can join, and that when it appears they will recognize it and unite.

And what is at stake? No generation that has come before us has ever had such a huge opportunity for greatness, simply because never before have the stakes been so high. But that also means that if you and I fail to act, ours will become the most vilified generation in human history, simply because we couldn't muster the will to change our ways, even though we understood the dire consequences of inaction. Our descendants will see that clearly.

But if we act, we will be honored as the Greatest Generation. We will redefine the words *hero* and *heroine*; and our descendants will boast of us as of kings and queens.

Back when the *Whole Earth Catalog* first came out I was an instant admirer. I later met its editor, Stewart Brand, when we worked together on *A Day for Whales* (an event decreed by then-Governor of California, Jerry Brown). What made the *Whole Earth Catalog* so valuable was that it brought together uniquely valuable information that was otherwise hard to access. When Lisa suggested that there ought to be a booklet for people who came to see our joint production, telling them how to get involved in what we'd talked about, I remembered how valuable Stewart Brand's first *Whole Earth Catalog* had been.

Her idea also reminded me of an excellent handbook whose practical suggestions had a wonderfully human dimension. It was called *50 Simple Things You Can Do to Save the Earth*—and it appeared in the 1980s. When Lisa called her book *What Can I Do?* I realized that it had been twenty years since answers to that question had been brought together in a single accessible place. I could see that by giving Internet references she would, in effect, be handing people the reference material they need to learn enough to act, and that would make her book a kind of *50 Simple Things You Can Do to Save the Earth* for the Internet age.

Action

Everything in this book is aimed at encouraging us to look at the way we live and how we might change it to embrace a more environmentally friendly lifestyle. Here are the sites of some organizations on the front lines of such change.

www.beyondpesticides.org

The National Coalition Against the Misuse of Pesticides informs the public about pesticides and safe alternatives. It works through local action within the community to effect change. Check out **Info Services** and **Emergencies**.

www.bluewaternetwork.org

The millions of two-stroke engines in the United States produce 1.1 billion pounds of toxic emissions annually. This organization is working to introduce cleaner four-stroke technology, and to solve environmental problems caused by cruise ships as well as other parts of the transport sector.

www.bluewaternetwork.org

At the age of twenty-four, **Russell Long** became the youngest skipper ever to compete in the America's Cup. He was the first person to break the fifty mile per hour barrier in a sailboat. But this world-class sailor is also an environmental activist, and while he was managing a fisheries project in Kerala, India, he discovered that the pollution from the two-stroke engines powering the fishermen's boats was so bad that the fish tasted like kerosene. Soon after, in 1996, Russell founded the **Bluewater Network**, an organization that campaigns to stop the serious water pollution caused by outboard engines and personal watercraft. He now also works to curb the destruction of ocean habitats by cruise ships, ferries, air and water pollution, and global warming. In 2000, *Boating Magazine* named Russell one of the marine industry's most influential people.

www.bucketbrigade.net

The Bucket Brigade. Are you worried that your family is being affected by chemicals released into the air by some local plant? This site tells you how to collect and analyze air samples using an affordable kit. Communities all over America are using this simple but effective way to discover what chemicals are in the air they breathe, where they come from, how they affect people, and what actions people can take to ensure enforcement of the applicable environmental laws. To get started, click on **Email us** and ask your questions.

www.citizen.org

Public Citizen works to protect consumer rights. It is active in such issues as health, auto safety, government accountability, social and economic justice, and environmental protection.

www.congress.org

Just enter your ZIP code to communicate with the president or your federal and state representatives about any issue that concerns you. See what others have written about, and how your representatives voted on particular issues.

www.ikecoalition.org

Improving Kids' Environment (IKE) uses its "right-to-know" agenda to learn about and reduce environmental threats to children's health. Families have the right to know about local environmental threats to their children.

www.labucketbrigade.org

The Louisiana Bucket Brigade is an environmental health and justice organization working with communities and their buckets to significantly reduce pollution produced by the state's oil refineries and chemical plants.

www.onesweetwhirled.org
Ben and Jerry's and Dave Matthews Band have joined forces with SaveOurEnvironment.org to tackle the issue of global warming and to show you how to become active in that fight.

www.pirg.org
Public Interest Research Groups. This organization keeps you informed about things going on in your state that are detrimental to your well-being, your health, and the health of your local environment. It helps you to change things for the better.

www.refineryreform.org
A national campaign working to cut pollution from America's oil refineries.

www.texasbucketbrigade.org
A group of neighborhoods in Texas using bucket technology to monitor the air they breathe. If you live near a source of air pollution in Texas, this group can help you fight for cleaner air.

www.thepetitionsite.com
A site that enables you to create or sign a petition in minutes, with links to concerned organizations.

Air

Air pollution is a growing problem. According to the Center for Disease Control and Prevention, asthma in the United States jumped by 75 percent between 1980 and 1994. Half of all Americans live in areas that don't meet federal clean air standards. The following sites will give you the information you need to clean up the air in your local community.

www.calcleanair.org
California Clean Air Campaign.

www.canarycoalition.org
A grassroots movement for clean air in North Carolina. Includes live camera views of national park sites, with daily air quality and ozone readings.

www.cleanairtrust.org
The Clean Air Trust. Check out the **Clean Air Villains** list.

www.cleanlungs.com
Citizens for Clean Air and Clean Lungs deals with the vexed question of smoking and works to make public facilities smoke free.

www.coalitionforcleanair.org
The Coalition for Clean Air in Southern California.

www.crp.cornell.edu/projects/southbronx
South Bronx Clean Air Coalition.

www.northtexasair.org
North Texas Clean Air Coalition.

❧ NATURAL LAWS ❧ INCLUDE SUCH SIMPLE TRUTHS AS THESE:

❧ To have a future, living things must live sustainably, producing only products that can be utilized by some other organism or broken down into inert components. ❧ No species living in a closed system can continue to expand its population indefinitely. (Just to be clear about this, Earth receives energy from the sun but is otherwise a closed system.) ❧ In order to survive, all species require some degree of stability in their habitat. ❧ The lives of every species including humans depend directly or indirectly on the lives of other species. ❧ All life, including human life, is a product of evolution and therefore selfish by its nature. Selfish behavior is an advantage to species until they dominate their closed system entirely, whereupon it becomes a fatal disadvantage—always. ❧

Just for the record, we in the developed world are currently out of step with every one of the above natural laws.

www.seedcoalition.org
Texans supporting clean air and clean energy.

www.wmcac.org
West Michigan Clean Air Coalition.

Architecture

www.mcdonough.com
Site for architect William McDonough (*Time* magazine's 1999 Hero of the Planet), who urges that we learn how to base our architectural designs on natural laws. He has said that a tree "makes oxygen, distills water, provides a habitat for hundreds of species, builds soil, uses solar energy as fuel, and self replicates. . . . What we are talking about is designing a building like a tree. That could actually happen."

Autos
(*See also* Transportation)

Cars are among the worst polluters on the planet. Whenever possible, carpool, use public transportation, and plan your daily activities to avoid unnecessary car trips. Consider hybrid or fuel cell technology for your next car.

www.bettersuv.org

A campaign run by SUV owners calling for safer, more fuel-efficient SUVs.

www.betterworldhandbook.com/ gasoline.html

See how "green" your gas provider is with this list of social responsibility ratings for gas stations.

www.carpoolconnect.com

Nationwide carpool information and networking.

www.carsharing.net

If you live in a city you don't need to own a car. This alternative provides 24-hour instant access to a network of cars, trucks, and vans that you can pick up and drop off in cities worldwide. Talk with experienced car sharers in **Carshare Café**.

www.clean-air.org

American Hydrogen Association. Want to convert your gas-guzzling ICE (internal combustion engine) to one that runs on hydrogen? The American Hydrogen Association provides a two-day course on how to do it. This site also contains lots of information on the new fuel cell technology.

www.epa.gov/greenvehicles/index.htm

The EPA's Green Vehicle Guide to environmental performance ratings.

www.evrental.com

America's first environmentally friendly car rental company.

www.hondacars.com

Click on the **Civic Hybrid** or on the **Insight**.

www.rmi.org

The Rocky Mountain Institute. Click on **Advanced Automotive News** to learn about alternative transportation technology and fuel-related issues.

www.toyota.com/prius

The most popular hybrid. Check your dealer's waiting list.

Batteries
(*See also* Cell Phones)

The batteries used by modern portable technology release some appalling toxins when discarded or incinerated. The better alternative is to recycle them.

www.rbrc.org
Rechargeable Battery Recycling Corporation will help you find drop-off sites near you.

Bicycles

www.bycyklen.dk/engelsk/frameset.html
Bicycling is healthy and helps prevent pollution. The citizens of Copenhagen have made 2,500 bicycles available for public use. Riders pay a refundable $3 deposit when picking up bikes from the program's bike stands. Could you do the same in your town or city?

Birds

www.audubon.org

In their efforts to preserve and restore natural ecosystems, the National Audubon Society focuses on birds. Learn about birds in your backyard. See a painting of your state bird in **Audubon's Birds of America**. Find out about West Nile Virus. Get involved in the **Christmas Bird Count**.

Books
(*See also* Paper)

To save forests, use your local library and share or donate books you've read.

❧ www.bookthing.org ❧

This small nonprofit developed from Russell Wattenberg's obsession to collect books from people who don't want them and give them away free to those who do—schools, people, children, anyone who wants them. Send all those surplus books to Russell.

www.chelseagreen.com

As the mass media empires grow exponentially, it has never been more important that the voice of the independent publisher be heard. Chelsea Green is a leading publisher of books on sustainable living and the new politics of the commons—the emerging voices of ordinary people worldwide as they begin to take back their water, their food, and the destruction of their land and housing from global corporations.

www.ecobooks.com
An alternative to Amazon. Eco Books is an online bookstore specializing in books covering ecological issues.

www.greenpressinitiative.org
Tyson Miller, who started the Green Press Initiative, states that the U.S. book publishing industry consumed 20 million trees in 2002 alone. This organization of authors and publishers is committed to using postconsumer recycled paper in all their publications.

www.islandpress.com
Island Press is an independent publisher of environmental books specializing in conservation biology, marine science, health, the economic profits in protecting ecosystems, and the exciting new solutions to environmental problems that are beginning to emerge.

www.worldashome.org
This site explores our relationship with the natural world through the lens of literature. Click on **Toward the Livable City** and add your literary contribution.

www.bookthing.org

Russell Wattenberg arrived in Baltimore in 1995 and started working at a local bar. During happy hour on Friday afternoons, teachers from local schools used to come and spend time at the bar. They talked to him of the difficulty of encouraging children to read when there was such a lack of books in the schools. Russell loved to read, and it irked him that children were being denied the chance to develop a passion for reading, so every week he began buying books in local thrift stores and giving them to the teachers for the children in their schools. The word spread, and soon people were coming from miles around with books that had been gathering dust in their homes and giving them to Russell for his "book thing." He set up a space in his basement to house them, called his project **The Book Thing,** and began giving away free the thousands of books he'd collected. Volunteers from his neighborhood came to build bookshelves and raised funds to help him set up a nonprofit, so that he could devote all his time to collecting and giving out books. In a typical weekend he will give away nearly ten thousand books and take in a similar number. **The Book Thing** grew out of Russell's love of reading. He loves to be surrounded by books. "Everybody's got to do something between the time they're born and the time they drop dead," he says. What he is doing is taking books that would have ended up in the dump, in the attic, unread and unloved, and giving them away to any child, any adult, any schoolteacher, any traveler, anyone who will give them a good home.

Building Green

www.buildinggreen.com
Provides building materials and an extensive library for aspiring and experienced green builders.

www.certifiedwood.org
Where to buy building products certified by the Forest Stewardship Council and SmartWood.

www.environmentalhomecenter.com
This Seattle company is a national distributor of green building materials.

www.greenfloors.com
Provides environmentally friendly flooring products and related information such as how to recycle your old flooring.

www.healthybuilding.net

A coalition of green building industry professionals, health activists, and environmentalists promoting the use of healthy building materials with the help of colleagues from the world of socially responsible investment.

www.notsobighouse.com

A site based on the book *The Not So Big House* by Sarah Susanka. Full of practical information and excellent links.

www.smartwood.org

SmartWood is an independent organization that certifies and promotes sustainably produced building materials.

Business

Going green in business is a crucial part of achieving sustainability.

www.carbohydrateeconomy.org

Carbohydrates can be used to make biodegradable products such as chemicals, paper, building materials, textiles, substitutes for plastic, and more. This technology produces less pollution, helps farmers, and is part of the closed-loop system.

www.ceres.org

The Coalition for Environmentally Responsible Economies provides a forum in which corporations, investment funds, environmental organizations, public interest groups, and communities can move toward sustainable living together.

www.greenbiz.com

"The Resource Center on Business, the Environment and the Bottom Line" is one of my favorite sites. It emphasizes how good environmental practices benefit the bottom line. Practical solutions and good news stories. Check out the **Toolbox**.

www.sustainablebusiness.com

The monthly newsletter provides information about investments in companies developing new ways of doing business.

The following three companies demonstrate that a successful international business can be based on a clear and central environmental vision:

www.interfacesustainability.com

Interface, Inc., is an award-winning, Fortune 500 company and a global leader in environmentally responsible manufacturing practices. By recycling carpets they demonstrate the principle of closed-loop systems with zero waste.

www.aveda.com

Sustainable beauty products. Aveda is a great example of an environmentally friendly business. Click on **Protect the Planet** and learn more.

www.sodra.com

When Södra Cell pioneered the development of chlorine-free pulp bleaching they were unconvinced of its importance to the environment. But when doing so made them the biggest pulp producer in Europe, they changed their outlook to pure green.

Cell Phones
(*See also* Batteries)

By 2005, up to 130 million cell phones may be thrown away in the United States each year. Instead of opting for the latest gizmos, use your cell phone as long as possible before buying another, and when you do replace it, be sure to give the old one to a good cause. To donate your old cell phone go to:

www.charitablerecycling.com
and
www.collectivegood.com

Children

www.checnet.org

The Children's Health Environmental Coalition informs parents about toxic threats to their children and what steps can be taken to stop them. Its board has included Erin Brockovich and Olivia Newton-John.

www.freshair.org

The Fresh Air Fund provides free summer vacations for children from inner-city communities in New York City, as guests of rural families or at a camp. Find out how to become a volunteer or a host family, or how to sign up your own child for a trip to the country.

www.healthyschools.org

Some schools have buildings or land that are unhealthy for the occupants. This site helps teachers, parents, and children find out how to make their schools healthier. It provides an excellent list of Internet resources, with downloadable reports and materials to help you improve the health of your school.

Circus

www.friendsofanimals.org/
animalfreecircus.html

Circuses that use animals often employ practices that are cruel to those animals. Check this site for a list of animal-free circuses that rely only on the amazing capabilities of the human animal.

Cleaning Products
(*See also* Vinegar)

Many cleaning products contain petrochemical components that are harmful to people, animals, and the environment. They degrade slowly, build up in the environment, and are toxic to aquatic life. Their production consumes high levels of energy, reduces the world's diminishing supply of petroleum, and causes irreparable environmental damage during oil drilling and extraction. Use biodegradable cleaning products that lack harmful petrochemicals, phosphates, and "active washing ingredients." Several companies make products that clean effectively and leave fewer harmful residues in the water and soil.

www.ecos.com

Earth Friendly Products. An award-winning manufacturer of environmentally friendly products.

www.seventhgeneration.com

Seventh Generation has won prizes for its attempts to preserve the environment. In my home state of Vermont, the company won the Governor's award.

Coffee

Deforestation to provide land for growing coffee destroys the trees in the wintering grounds of migratory songbirds. Support companies that produce and sell shade-grown coffee, cultivated under a forest canopy that preserves the natural habitat needed for migratory songbirds and other creatures. In four thousand locations across America Dunkin' Donuts now uses only fair trade coffee for their espresso-based drinks.

www.equalexchange.org

Buy fair trade coffee directly from small-scale farmer co-ops in Africa, Asia, and Latin America.

www.groundsforchange.com
and
www.greenmountaincoffee.com

Two places to buy fair trade coffee from socially responsible companies on the Web.

http://magazine.audubon.org/features0408/mexico.html

An article about shade-grown coffee and birds that taught me a lot.

www.robustion.ca

This company makes Java-Logs—recycled coffee grounds pressed into high-energy, clean-burning logs.

www.starbucks.com/aboutus/compost
Starbucks will give you their coffee grounds for
your compost heap or the worms in your worm
bin, who will find them delicious (provided they
are mixed with other vegetable matter). Speak to
the manager of your local Starbucks.

Communication

Help build a world that is cleaner, safer, more fair,
and ultimately better every time you use your
credit card or make a long-distance call.

www.earthtones.com
Earth Tones is wholly owned by a nonprofit environmental organization. It donates 100 percent of
its profits to environmental advocacy and organ-
izing. Its monthly bills are printed on recycled
paper. It also lets you make free calls to Congress.

www.workingassets.com
Working Assets provides credit cards and long-
distance telephone accounts, and donates a por-
tion of its revenue to nonprofit groups working
for peace, human rights, equality, education, and
the environment.

Community

www.care2.com

To build a community you need to be connected. This compendium of sites offers news, environmental information, shopping, jokes, and free cards, plus an active online community offering discussion groups, photo swapping, and companionship. Get connected!

www.newrules.org

The Institute of Local Self-Reliance provides this resource for activists, policymakers, and organizations working with communities to revive their economic base.

www.simpleliving.net

Another cyberspace community. Let the hundreds of links on this site help you live a simpler and perhaps happier life.

Compost

(*See also* Coffee, Gardens, Trash, *and* Worms)

http://journeytoforever.org/compost.html

Compost your household food waste and see how your garden grows. This site provides all the information you need to get started.

Composting Toilets

Fresh water is rapidly becoming a scarce natural resource. Flushing of toilets may be using as much as 5 percent of available fresh water. Composting toilets use little or no water, have no connection to sewage systems, and produce an end product that is safe, healthful, and beneficial to gardens.

www.altenergystore.com
Tells you where to buy composting toilets. Click on **Composting Toilets** at the bottom of the page.

www.compostingtoilet.org/explain.cfm
Explains how these toilets work.

www.falconwaterfree.com
Odor-free, waterless urinals for schools and public buildings that can save forty thousand gallons of fresh water per fixture annually. Clients already include the City of Beverley Hills, Daimler-Chrysler, Everglades National Park, Ford Motor Corporation, IBM, Las Vegas Motor Speedway, Johnson and Johnson, the U.S. Marine Corps, the Rosebowl, Six Flags Amusement Park, and many American universities.

Conscious Consumerism

www.ecomall.com

Stroll through the Earth's largest mall—a mall that deals only in "green"!

www.gaiam.com

A provider of information, goods, and services about the environment, sustainable living, healthy lifestyles, alternative health care, and personal development.

www.greenculture.com

This site offers a comprehensive selection of goods for the home made from recycled materials, ecologically harvested timber, and other Earth-friendly components.

www.igive.com

Buy things online and give a percentage of what you pay for each item to your favorite charity.

www.pbs.org/kcts/affluenza

It has been said that Americans, who make up only 5 percent of the world's population, use nearly a third of its resources and produce almost half of its hazardous waste. *Affluenza* is a one-hour film that explores the high costs of consumerism to our society and environment. It shows men and women across the country who have decided to spend more time with friends and family and not allow the drive to acquire more things to dominate their lives. This site analyzes the problems of over-consumption, with good suggestions for treatment. Learn about the film, order it, download discussion guides, and plan an evening sharing it with your friends.

www.responsibleshopper.org
Compare and contrast the different environmental and social policies that underlie the companies you buy from and the services you use.

✿ FOR THE SHOPPER ✿
IN ALL OF US:

✿ Shop more consciously. ✿ Rethink purchases. ✿ Do I really need it? ✿ Can I borrow, rent, or buy it locally? ✿ Is it sustainably produced? ✿ How long will it last? ✿ Is its competitor cheaper to recycle? ✿

Consumer Web Watch

www.consumerwebwatch.com
The Consumer Web Watch is a service provided by the Consumer's Union to help you monitor the accuracy of information published on the Internet.

Coral Reefs

Coral reefs are among the world's most endangered yet most productive ecosystems. They have worldwide economic significance. But coral reefs everywhere are being destroyed by multiple forces: global warming, which causes bleaching; pollution from agricultural runoff and human wastes; sedimentation from coastal development, dredging, deforestation, and bad agricultural practices; and over-harvesting, largely because of illegal fishing techniques that use dynamite to catch food fish and cyanide to catch aquarium fish.

Lobby governments to support treaties and international agreements protecting this irreplaceable treasure. Avoid buying wild-caught, tropical, saltwater aquarium fish. Support companies, such as PetCo, that sell only artificial coral for aquariums. If you're a diver or snorkeler, learn techniques that don't harm coral reefs.

Sites for good information about coral reefs and the stresses they face:

www.coralreef.noaa.gov
and
www.epa.gov/owow/oceans/coral

Democracy

www.democracyforamerica.com

This organization, started by Howard Dean, provides support for those who wish to stand for office at all levels of government, and is building the network to help those candidates succeed.

www.lwv.org

The League of Women Voters, a nonpartisan grassroots citizen organization, can help you understand major policy issues and get you engaged in the democratic process on the local, state, and federal levels. It supports equal rights for all and social and economic justice. The **Interactive Center** will lead you to your representatives.

www.nfrw.org

The National Federation of Republican Women encourages women of all ages to become involved in the political process.

Diapers

Every year in the United States, up to 4.4 million metric tons of non-biodegradable diapers go into landfills. For biodegradable or reusable diapers, visit the following sites:

www.organicbebe.com
and
www.diaperaps.com

Dry Cleaning

www.earth911.org/usa/master
.asp?s=lib&a=shopsmart/tech.html
Learn about wet cleaning, a healthy alternative to dry cleaning.

www.greenearthcleaning.com
This company has developed a gentler, healthier way to dry-clean clothes, using a biodegradable, silicon-based solvent that has no lingering odor.

www.laundry-alternative.com/noperc.html
An article about the hazards of the dry cleaning process.

Educating Yourself

If we want our children to inherit a healthy planet, we must realize that our individual actions matter, and we must start making educated and responsible decisions. In order to make those decisions, we need reliable information.

Start Here:

www.bioneers.org

The Bioneers include scientists and artists, gardeners and economists, teachers and public servants, architects and ecologists, farmers and journalists, priests and shamans, policymakers, students, and everyday people. Their annual conference is a focal point for the visionary, yet practical solutions that human ingenuity is spawning to restore the living systems of Earth.

www.earthisland.org

The Earth Island Institute supports over thirty grassroots projects that are working to help conserve and restore Earth's threatened biodiversity and natural systems.

www.eco-portal.com

The gateway to in-depth worldwide environmental information. Good for a rainy afternoon.

www.environmentaldefense.org

Environmental Defense does just that. Since 1967 its team of scientists, lawyers, and economists has worked to ensure clean air, healthy water, a rich biosphere, and a better future for life on Earth. They have shared such successes as phasing out the lead in gas and establishing safe drinking water standards. Check out **Partnerships** to see what they are doing with companies like FedEx and McDonald's.

www.ewg.org

The Environmental Working Group is a research organization that uses the power of accurate information to improve public and environmental health. Check out what they say about **Teflon**.

www.ifaw.org

The International Fund for Animal Welfare believes that the interests of animals and humans are not separate. The organization was the chief supporter of the complex science that resulted in a moratorium on whaling. For three decades they have fought to stop the harp seal hunt in Canada. Along with the National Resources Defense Council (NRDC), IFAW was at the center of the fight that successfully prevented construction of the world's largest manufacturing facility in one of the most protected conservation areas on Earth, Laguna San Ignacio in Mexico.

www.newdream.org

The Center for a New American Dream encourages responsible consumption and works to shift America away from over-consumption toward a more fulfilling, just, and sustainable way of life. Click on **Turn the Tide**. Go to **Partners** to look for environmental organizations in your region.

www.nrdc.org

Through lawsuits, the Natural Resources Defense Council has become one of the nation's most effective environmental action organizations. They shared in the successful defense of San Ignacio Bay with IFAW.

www.rmi.org

The Rocky Mountain Institute is one of the premier nonprofit environmental organizations in the United States. It works with governments, communities, businesses, and individuals to reshape economies. Click on **Natural Capitalism; Energy; Transportation; Water;** and **Climate**. Explore the **Bookstore; Education and Outreach;** and **Newsletter**.

www.saveourenvironment.org
Get in touch with many of the environmental advocacy groups working to heal the planet.

www.sierraclub.org
The Sierra Club is one of America's largest grass-roots environmental organizations. Click on **My Backyard** to connect with a Sierra Club group in your state. Make new friends, go on hikes, learn about creatures living near you, and work with others to improve the health of the land, rivers, streams, and air in your region.

Going Deeper:

www.earth-policy.org
Lester Brown, one of our most influential thinkers, sets out his vision for an environmentally sustainable economy.

www.lcv.org
The League of Conservation Voters (LCV) keeps a nonpartisan, environmental voting record on the activities of representatives in all three branches of government.

www.ucsusa.org
Union of Concerned Scientists. A source of excellent information about threats we all face.

www.worldwatch.org
Their annual *State of the World Report* is a classic.

Deeper Still:

www.nationalacademies.org/nrc
The reports of the National Research Council (NRC) are the government's major source of reliable scientific, engineering, and medical information. When inviting experts to write a report, the Academies make every effort to balance biases, so that the finished report will reflect only what is truly known about a subject. The government retains no right to approve either the experts or their reports.

Endangered Species

Loss of species is a useful measure of human impact on Earth's biodiversity. Learn more about what we are losing.

www.batcon.org
Though bats are almost universally feared and vilified, they offer humans vast benefits by eating insects and pollinating plants. Bat Conservation International has shown extraordinary intelligence and effect in protecting bats. Build or buy one of their bat boxes.

www.cites.org

The Convention on International Trade in Endangered Species of Wild Flora and Fauna is one of the most effective laws we have for protecting endangered species.

www.defenders.org

Defenders of Wildlife works to protect native plants and animals from becoming endangered through loss of habitat.

www.endangeredspecie.com

Provides lists of the endangered species in your state.

www.iucnredlist.org

The IUCN Red Data Book and Red List are the ultimate authorities on what species now need protection from humans.

www.rhinos-irf.org

Fewer than 17,500 rhinos are alive in the wild today. Some species are down to just a handful of survivors. The International Rhino Foundation works to protect those that are left.

www.savingcranes.org

There is wide agreement that several species of cranes owe their survival to the efforts of the International Crane Foundation.

www.wcs.org

The Wildlife Conservation Society has one of the oldest and most distinguished records in endangered species conservation. It is because of this organization that we still have bison in America.

www.well.com/user/davidu/extinction.html

Telling it like it is. This site, a comprehensive source of information on the mass extermination of species, is an altogether sobering experience.

www.wwfus.org

The World Wildlife Fund has taken the lead in countless conservation efforts.

www.xerces.org

Using advocacy, public outreach, and research, the Xerces Society works to protect endangered bees, butterflies, and other invertebrates, as well as their habitats.

Energy

"No other issue intersects with a wider variety of environmental problems than what kind of energy we employ to empower society, where we get it, and how efficiently we use it." —*Earth Day Guide to Planet Repair*

As consumers, we must demand renewable

energy. The power begins with us. Call your utility and ask for it. If enough of us do, the collective impact on the production of cheap, renewable energy will be enormous and more will become more available.

www.aceee.org

American Council for an Energy-Efficient Economy. On this site you can buy two informative booklets: *A Consumer Guide to Home Energy Savings* and *The Most Energy-Efficient Appliances.*

http://amconservationgroup.com

Here's where your local co-op, book-reading group, church, school, office, and hardware store can buy energy-saving products in bulk online.

www.apolloalliance.org

Inspired by JFK's Apollo Project to put a man on the moon, the Apollo Alliance—a coalition of people from labor, environmental, business, and faith communities—aims to create three million new jobs, invest in renewable energy technology to end our dependence on OPEC, and work for a healthier environment.

www.ase.org

The Alliance to Save Energy is a coalition of business, government, environmental, and consumer leaders that supports and advocates energy efficiency through education and research. Check out the list in their **Powerful $avings Campaign.** For a virtual tour of their energy-efficient Washington office, go to **www.ase.org/content/article/detail/1036.**

www.awea.org

The American Wind Energy Association provides detailed information on wind energy technology, installation of systems small and large, and the development of the industry worldwide.

www.cleanair-coolplanet.org

CA-CP is a science-based organization in the Northeast that works with businesses, governments, communities, faith-based groups, and college campuses to find affordable, practical, and effective solutions to global warming.

www.dsireusa.org

The Database of State Incentives for Renewable Energy. Information on state and selected federal incentives that promote renewable energy. Explore their **School Going Solar** program and find out about small wind turbine projects.

www.eere.energy.gov/greenpower/buying

Find out whether you can buy green power from your supplier and how that buying process works. Invest in the development of renewable energy for your community and protect your air, water, and health. The **Map of Green Pricing Programs** links you to nationwide information about utilities offering green power.

www.energyfuturecoalition.org

The Energy Future Coalition is led by Boyden Gray, former Counsel to President George H. W. Bush; John Podesta, President Clinton's former Chief of Staff; and former CIA Director James Woolsey. The coalition advocates investment in alternative energy technologies to end U.S. dependence on foreign oil as a matter of national security. Check out *The Day After Tomorrow* Facts.

www.energystar.gov

Energy Star is a government-backed program helping businesses and individuals to protect the environment through more efficient uses of energy.

www.nativeenergy.com

Develops domestic renewable energy resources in partnership with Native American groups. Their first project was a wind farm for the Rosebud Sioux Tribe in South Dakota, and they are now concentrating on building small wind farms on many more Native American lands. Wind farms are likely to become a major future source of income for Native Americans.

www.nesea.org/energy/info

The North East Sustainable Energy Association is a good place to discover how you can generate or buy clean energy, what it costs, and the financial benefits you can expect.

www.realgoods.com

On this extensive site you can buy a solar charger for your cell phone, an off-grid refrigerator, supplies for solar and wind power technology, a solar-powered multi-band radio, and many other ecologically sustainable products.

www.resource-solutions.org

Based in San Francisco, the Center for Resource Solutions has a number of programs focusing on national and international renewable energy issues. Their **Marketers' Marketers Group** provides a forum for those selling alternative energy. Their **Green-e Program** helps consumers find certified sources of renewable power.

Fair Trade

Fair Trade is a means of guaranteeing that artisans and farmers are paid fairly for what they make and grow. Fair trade promotes community development, health, child care, education, and environmental stewardship. Make a resolution to shift a percentage of the money you spend each month on gifts, housewares, toys, and coffee to fair trade products. Ask your local businesses to carry fair trade products and when they do, let them know that you appreciate it. For further information go to:

www.co-opamerica.org
and
www.fairtradefederation.org

Faith-Based Initiatives

www.coejl.org
The Coalition on the Environment and Jewish Life promotes environmental education, scholarship, advocacy, and action in the American Jewish community.

**www.epa.gov/smallbiz/archive/
congregations102902.html**

Energy Star for Congregations. The EPA's voluntary Energy Star program helps your church reduce energy costs.

www.gis.net/~rwe

Religious Witness for the Earth.

www.ncccusa.org

Uniting congregations from many different religious communities across America, the National Council of Churches involves itself in a broad range of issues including the environment, poverty, and racism.

www.theregenerationproject.org

The Regeneration Project is an interfaith ministry that celebrates the deep connection between faith and ecology. Its primary focus is combating global warming. Explore this site, and if you feel this is something your church community might like to be involved with, click on **Interfaith Power and Light** for more information.

Get involved locally through the following sites:

www.emoregon.org/INEC.htm

Ecumenical Ministries of Oregon.

www.gipl.org
Georgia Interfaith Power and Light.

www.ipandl.org
Pennsylvania Interfaith Power and Light.

www.meipl.org
Maine Interfaith Power and Light.

www.mipandl.org
Massachusetts Interfaith Power and Light (has wonderful links).

Farming
(*See also* Food *and* Meat)

**www.commondreams.org/
views02/0729-01.htm**
A *Los Angeles Times* article about the death of productive land from industrialized farming.

www.farmland.org
American Farmland Trust encourages stewardship of American farms and farmland. Their annual $10,000 Steward of the Land Award goes to a farm family that works hard at protecting the land and the environment. At the bottom of their home page, see their film, *Imagine the Earth as an Apple*.

www.grassfarmer.com

A site focusing on Cove Mountain Farm, a project of the American Farmland Trust that demonstrates that grass farmers can flourish in small properties near urban areas—proof that there is an alternative to the philosophy of "get big or get out" that has destroyed so many family farms.

www.nal.usda.gov/afsic/csa/

Information about Community Supported Agriculture (CSAs) from the Alternative Farming Systems Information Center.

www.naturallygrown.org

Certified Naturally Grown™, used by small farmers who sell their products locally, is the grassroots alternative to the USDA's National Organic Program. You can register your farm and apply for certification on this site.

www.pmac.net/AM/no_blackouts.html

An article from *American Farm Bureau News* on the benefits of converting methane from manure to electricity.

Films

www.bullfrogfilms.com

The leading U.S. distributor of environmental videos. Over five hundred titles—great stuff.

www.freerangegraphics.com

Free Range Graphics makes witty, animated films addressing environmental issues. Share them with friends.

Fish

(*See also* Seafood)

Eating farmed fish that have a vegetable diet, such as tilapia, catfish, and crawfish, is preferable to eating farmed shrimp or salmon, which require a diet of smaller, wild-caught fish.

**www.ewg.org/issues/mercury/
20031209/calculator.php**

This simple calculator lets you find out how much tuna you can safely eat each week. For children and women of childbearing age this calculator is critical.

http://seafood.audubon.org
and
www.mbayaq.org/cr/seafoodwatch.asp

These two sites offer downloadable wallet-card guides that show you what species of fish are best to eat and why. Print out multiple copies for your friends. I use one whenever I buy fish, in both restaurants and fish markets.

Flowers

www.laborrights.org

Click on **Fairness in Flowers Campaign** to learn about health and safety issues in the flower industry.

www.organicbouquet.com

An online source for organic flowers, fruits, and gift baskets.

Food

(See also Meat *and* Seafood)

Eating wholesome food is one of the most effective ways to stay healthy, but one we sometimes forget. It makes sense to avoid foods treated with pesticides, hormones, antibiotics, and chemical fertilizers. An easy first step to better health is to buy fresh, locally grown produce.

www.chefscollaborative.org

A national network of more than one thousand members of the food community who promote sustainable cuisine. Members are given excellent, in-depth information to help them make environmentally sound decisions about the food they serve. Partnerships with local farmers are encouraged. You can find a list of member restaurants on this site.

www.commondreams.org/
views03/0123-09.htm
A different view of how we often choose to eat. The article "Fast Food Fascism" speculates that the fast food movement could be affecting the American spirit of rugged individualism.

www.eatwild.com
Find out about the problems inherent in the feedlot method of raising animals, and the benefits of antibiotic-free, grass-fed, and organic meat. You can find in-depth information based on scientific studies (for farmers as well as consumers) about grass-fed and organic beef, bison, lamb, poultry, and dairy products. Pasture-based farmers can register to sell their products from this site.

www.foodnews.org
Pesticides are not meant for human consumption. Click on **Produce** and download "The Shopper's Guide to Pesticides," a handy wallet card to help you choose produce that will lower your exposure to pesticides. I use this card whenever I'm shopping.

www.localharvest.org
Check out the good foods you can buy from family farms in your area. Click on **Partnerships**

for links to information on sustainable agriculture nationwide. If you are a farmer, a market manager, or the owner of a locally grown food-related business, you can add your listing to their directory for free.

www.loe.org/favorites/foods.htm
A list of the top ten foods you should avoid unless they have been grown organically.

www.safe-food.org
A short course on genetically modified foods.

www.slowfoodusa.org
The opposite of fast food. Everything here celebrates the pleasure of eating in a leisurely fashion and the wealth of tastes available to us. Slow Food U.S.A. is putting the dining table back into the center of our lives, and its education program is introducing schoolchildren all over America to the delights of growing and cooking their own food.

www.sustainabletable.org
An excellent site offering information about food choices that are healthy for both you and the environment.

www.sustainabletable.org/shop/csa
Community Supported Agriculture is a way to buy vegetables from your local growers. Your support will help them survive, while you will

save energy and cut back on the pollution created when food is shipped hundreds of miles from a producer to your table. Your food will be fresher and therefore healthier.

Formal Dresses

www.glassslipperproject.org
That bridesmaid's dress hanging in the back of your closet could transform a young girl's sense of self during one of the most important moments of her life. The Glass Slipper Project in Chicago provides junior and senior high school girls of limited means the chance to shine at their school proms. With the help of volunteers and donations of formal dresses, accessories, and unopened makeup, this organization gives young women a formal dress and all that goes with it, including the self-esteem.

www.glassslipperproject.org/yostate.htm
For similar organizations throughout America.

Fuel Cells

www.fuelcells.org
The Online Fuel Cell Information Center gives a good introduction to fuel cell technology—the energy of the future.

Gardens

(See also Pollinators)

You can begin to heal the Earth in your own backyard by making a garden, growing your own fruit, flowers, and vegetables, and providing a home for pollinators, the insects without whom we would have no fruit, flowers, or vegetables.

www.gardeners.com

Run by gardeners, this Vermont company provides a comprehensive list of tested, Earth-friendly gardening supplies. Advice, seeds, garden furniture, homes for birds, healthy pest control techniques (such as barley balls for clearing algae from your pond), and tomato plants that grow upside down!

www.greeninggotham.org

Imagine every rooftop in NYC transformed into a garden or a meadow of wildflowers. Greening Gotham advocates a solution to some of the urgent environmental challenges facing New York City through cultivation of rooftop gardens.

www.highmowingseeds.com
A certified organic seed company that supplies seeds in small or bulk amounts for gardeners and farmers. Retailers can order seed racks from the company, and gardeners can download planting and seed saving information.

www.newenglandnatural.com/wildfl.html
For pure wildflower seed (no added fillers).

www.seedsofchange.com
Organic seeds, books, starting your garden, growing garlic, questions answered, employment opportunities, fruit trees and vines, organic fruit gift boxes, and a seed donation program are some of the many pleasures of this site.

www.seedsource.com
Native American Seed is a Texan family company dealing solely in plants endemic to their region. Seeds from native plants, wildflowers, and prairie grasses, planted in their natural habitats, grow and thrive without needing extra water or fertilizer. By using native plants in your garden, you'll support the pollinators and wildlife that depend on them, and your garden will be more ecologically friendly.

www.seedstrust.com

A family-owned company in the mountains of Central Idaho dedicated to collecting, conserving, and producing seeds. They specialize in short-season, cold-tolerant plants. Their collection includes tomatoes from Siberia, carrots from Mount Fuji, and wild poppies from Iceland. Click on the **Seed Saving** link for downloadable instructions about harvesting your own seeds to grow next season.

www.xeriscape.org

How to grow a beautiful garden with limited access to water. Go to **Xeriscape Maintenance Journal** for other links.

Gifts

(*See also* Heifer Project)

www.whatgoesaround.org

A nonprofit organization that offers an entirely novel approach to both giving and receiving gifts. If you don't want any more stuff, go to this site and list the charities you would like friends to contribute to in your name. If you can't afford to donate to charity, this site gives you a way to do so, but at no cost to yourself.

Global Warming

The Earth is heating up. By burning fossil fuels and clear-cutting forests, humans are adding carbon dioxide and other heat-trapping greenhouse gases to the atmosphere at a perilous rate. The consequences of global warming are potentially catastrophic. You can help change the situation.

www.climateark.org/vital
This site clearly lays out the causes and effects of climate change from global warming. For every picture or graphic you see here double click on it to get the full impact. Then go to the **Climate Ark Home Page** for information from all over the world about the effects of global warming.

www.climatestar.org
Information on the causes of global warming, its impact, and potential solutions.

www.epa.gov/globalwarming
The global warming site run by the Environmental Protection Agency.

http://undoit.org/undoit_steps_1.cfm
Twenty simple steps you can take to help undo global warning.

Golf

Golf courses traditionally consume masses of fresh water and need huge amounts of fertilizers and pesticides to stay "healthy." The subsequent runoff pollutes the groundwater, streams, rivers, and lakes. Now some in the golf industry are working to reverse the environmental blight of these playgrounds.

**www.auduboninternational.org/
programs/signature/members**
A national list of golf courses that include sustainable practices in their management.

www.committedtogreen.com
This campaign, started by the European Golf Association Ecology Unit, encourages the environmental improvement of golf courses through conservation of biodiversity and water, sustainable development of new courses, energy conservation, and minimization of waste.

www.usga.org/turf
United States Golf Association. Click on **Environmental Programs** and see how the Audubon Society and the USGA are combining to lower the environmental impact of golf courses. The **Wildlife Links Program** explores the connection between golf and the wild world.

Green Pages

www.greenpages.org

Co-op America's Green Pages is a treasure trove of resources for socially responsible investing, community building, green products of all kinds, eco-travel, tree-free paper, sustainably produced furniture, and much more.

Health

www.afhh.org

The Alliance for Healthy Homes started out working to protect children from the poisonous effects of lead, and now covers all aspects of health hazards in the home. Offers a good list of resources.

www.castingforrecovery.org

Free fly-fishing weekend retreats for breast cancer survivors. Provides counseling, the opportunity to make new friends, and a chance to learn how to fly fish using the **Catch-and-Release** program.

www.come-clean.org

Coming Clean was created after the PBS broadcast of Bill Moyers's documentary *Trade Secrets*, which exposed how the chemical industry is marketing products without sufficiently testing them for their effects on public health and safety. Click on **Ten Reasons** to see why we should be concerned about this issue.

http://ehp.niehs.nih.gov
Environmental Health Perspectives provides up-to-date, peer-reviewed research and news on environmental issues affecting your health.

www.ewg.org/reports/skindeep
Assess the safety of the ingredients in your regular skin and hair products on the Environmental Working Group's cosmetic safety list.

www.ourstolenfuture.org
The book *Our Stolen Future* draws the world's attention to the serious problems that some manufactured chemicals are causing to the developing fetus. Scientific studies show that these endocrine disrupters are affecting both humans and wildlife. This site introduces you to the ideas discussed in the book, helps you to understand those ideas, connects you to the most up-to-date information, and offers suggestions about what you as a consumer can do to minimize the risk of exposure to these hormonally disruptive contaminants.

www.psr.org
Winner of the 1985 Nobel Prize for Peace, Physicians for Social Responsibility brings together citizens and physicians to fight for public policies that protect human health and safety.

www.silentspring.org

This partnership of scientists, physicians, public health advocates, and community activists works to identify—and then to change—the ways in which pollution and the environment impact women's health. They are especially concerned with the environmental causes and prevention of breast cancer.

www.smallstep.gov

A site run by the Department of Health and Human Services. It encourages us to take small steps to lose the extra weight that threatens our health.

www.worstpills.org

Public Citizen's Health Research Group runs this site, which gives you the latest information on prescription and over-the-counter drugs and dietary supplements. Public Citizen accepts no funding from interested parties, so the information is objective and independent. Receive e-mail alerts about drug dangers, learn about generic drugs, and report adverse drug reactions to the FDA.

Heifer Project

www.heifer.org

The Heifer Project believes that by donating animals to people in need, you can help them feed themselves, and through sustainable farming, help them produce more animals to feed their community. If you're looking for a special gift, explore this site. I've purchased many Christmas presents here.

Hiking

Healthier than driving for you and the planet.

www.americanhiking.org

The American Hiking Society builds and maintains walking trails all over the United States. Check out the **Top Ten Family Trails**. Find both a trail and a trail club near you.

www.peaktopeak.net

An international compendium of walking and backpacking sites. Use the links to hiking clubs worldwide to find a local walking companion.

Home
(*See also* Wastes, Hazardous)

www.beyondpesticides.org/main.html
For information about pest management, click on **Safety Sources for Pest Management**.

www.energyhawk.com
This simple and very informative site was created by a husband and wife team in Seattle after they became concerned about the effect of rising energy costs on family budgets. The site is clearly laid out and full of great tips to save both energy and money.

www.greenchoices.com
Excellent links to help you make green choices for everything you do or use in your home and office.

www.greenfeet.com
Want a stainless steel refillable water bottle to help get plastic ones out of your life? How about plates made from recycled glass? A lavender heat wrap to sooth your tense neck? A CD holder made from hemp? All these and much more. Plus a gift registry that allows several friends to share the cost of one big purchase.

www.greenhome.com

Fifteen people in a garage in San Francisco, linked by the Internet to others across the country, have made this an attractive and user-friendly site where you can explore anything you might want to know about making your home a healthier place to live. Check out the comprehensive **Toxipedia**, take the **Healthy Home Tour**, buy in bulk for your office or your next big party, see why an LCD monitor is healthier for you and the environment, and buy biodegradable plates made from the stalks of sugarcane! They have a rigorous product-approval policy for everything they sell. They answered my e-mailed questions helpfully and promptly.

www.greenmatters.com

The Busy Person's Guide to Greener Living is for the multi-taskers among us. Get answers to your questions, great links, and an excellent assortment of books. Click on **Tune In** to listen to environmental radio stations.

www.greenseal.org/recommendations.htm

For an independent, science-based, detailed assessment of green products for your home and office. If a product has the Green Seal, it's safe and healthy for you and the environment.

http://householdproducts
.nlm.nih.gov/index.htm

The Household Products database of the National Institute of Health can give you information about the potential chemical hazards lurking in over five thousand household products under your kitchen sink and in your bathroom, laundry, and garage.

www.thegreenguide.com

The Green Guide Institute is a nonprofit research group that educates consumers about the environmental, health, and social impacts of their day-to-day decisions. They produce *The Green Guide*, which you can download (a savings in paper and postage). You can also participate in one of their Green Guide Research Panels.

www.thegreenguide.com/community

Click on **Just Ask** for in-depth answers to questions about socially responsible banking, how to eliminate toxic residues in your garden, how to dispose of your old toaster, and nontoxic ways to clear a blocked drain.

www.theorganicreport.org

This very informative site makes the case for why you should seriously consider an organic lifestyle for yourself and your family.

Hunting and Fishing

We all owe a lot to people who fish and hunt responsibly, with respect for wild animals and their habitats. The following is a list of hunting and fishing associations that place conservation of wildlife habitat and humane, sustainable hunting practices at the forefront of their activities.

www.boone-crockett.org/index.asp

The Boone and Crockett Club, founded by Theodore Roosevelt in 1887, published the first ethical code for sportsmen promoting the judicious management of big game. They have an extensive conservation education program.

www.conservamerica.org

Seeks to engage those who are traditionally more conservative—such as hunters, fishermen, and ranchers—in the battle for a healthier environment.

www.ducks.org

Ducks Unlimited is the world's largest waterfowl and wetlands conservation organization. Without their work there would be only remnant populations of ducks and geese in North America.

www.eco-hunt.co.za

An elephant eco-hunt in Africa that ends with the hunter granting, rather than taking, the elephant's life.

www.elkfoundation.org

Elk Foundation.

www.grousepartners.org

North American Grouse Partnership.

www.iwla.org

The Izaak Walton League works to protect the nation's soil, air, woods, waters, and wildlife.

www.joincca.org

The Coastal Conservation Association is for salt-water fishers.

www.muledeer.org

The Mule Deer Foundation.

http://news.nationalgeographic.com/news/ 2003/06/0616_030616_greenhunting.html

Read about a new kind of big game hunting in Africa. The hunter gets a trophy (not just a photograph!) and the animal lives.

www.nwtf.org

National Wild Turkey Federation.

www.pheasantsforever.org
Pheasants Forever.

www.tu.org
Trout Unlimited works nationwide to restore and preserve trout and salmon fisheries and their habitats.

www.vermejoparkranch.com/Ecology.php
Ted Turner's Vermejo Park Ranch has an extensive ecosystem and species restoration program. Hunt and fish on one of the last vast tracts of the Wild West.

www.whitetailsunlimited.com
Deer hunting.

Investment

Socially Responsible Investment is the commitment to invest in companies, products, and services that are economically, environmentally, and socially responsible.

www.calvertfoundation.org
Supports affordable housing, minority lending, microcredit, small business, and social enterprise programs around the world. Request a free **Community Investing Kit**.

www.ecomall.com/biz/menus.htm
For objective advice on where to find green investments.

www.shareholderaction.org
Shows you how to use your power as a shareholder to effect social and environmental change.

www.socialinvest.org
Comprehensive information, contacts, and resources on socially responsible investing.

www.trilliuminvest.com
Claims to be the oldest and largest independent investment firm dedicated to socially responsible investments.

Jobs

Many of the sites in this book offer employment opportunities.

www.greenbiz.com/jobs
A clearing house for green jobs and careers. You can post your resumé here.

Junk Mail

Less than 20 percent of all junk mail is recycled. Annually, more than 4 million tons end up in landfills. That's 340,000 garbage trucks every year filled to the brim with nothing but junk mail.

**www.environmentaldefense.org/
alliance/catalogs_tips.html**
Take control of the avalanche of catalogs in your mailbox. Stop those unwanted mailings here.

www.newdream.org/junkmail/form.html
Remove your name from unwanted mailing lists
here. Or do it by sending a letter to:

Mail Preference Service
c/o Direct Marketing Association
PO Box 9008,
Farmingdale, NY 11735-9008

Include the date, your name, address, and signa-
ture, along with the message: "Please register my
name with the Mail Preference Service."

Keep America Beautiful

Litter is an eyesore, a pollutant, and a hazard to your health. Working with like-minded individuals during neighborhood "Green Up" campaigns can make cleaning up fun. When taking a walk, carry a trash bag and fill it with litter as you go. Bending over to pick up trash adds to the fitness benefits of your walk, and improves your view on your next walk! (Gloves are a good idea.)

www.kab.org
The nation's largest community cleanup network. Click on **Toolbox** for ideas to help you organize your own hometown cleanup.

Keystone Species

Keystone species are fundamental to the survival of the ecosystem in which they live. If such a species is eliminated from its habitat, the ecosystem will eventually collapse.

www.prairiedogs.org/keystone.html

Blacktailed prairie dogs are considered a pest. This site demonstrates that as a keystone species they are essential to the survival of the prairie ecosystem.

**www.savethegreatbear.org/
CAD/Salmon.htm**

Not only do salmon feed bears, wolves, eagles, and otters, but their dead bodies also provide fertilizer for the forests that shade the streams in which the salmon spawn and those animals live. Find out more about the interconnection of species in a specific habitat on this site.

Laundry

TO SAVE ENERGY AND LOWER YOUR ELECTRIC BILL:

☙ Wash your laundry at the lowest possible recommended temperature, even cold. ☙ Don't waste water and energy washing lots of small loads. ☙ Use a clothes-line for drying as often as possible. ☙ To extend your machine's life and functionability, run it empty every two to three months on a warm cycle, using white vinegar instead of detergent. ☙

www.aceee.org
Information on the most energy-efficient appliances to choose.

www.laundrylist.org
Project Laundry List offers everything you need to do the laundry, and encourages you to use the sun as an energy-saving clothes dryer. Click on

Library to find something to read while you wait for the clothes to dry.

Lighting
(*See also* Energy *and* Home)

A compact fluorescent light bulb (CFL) lasts up to thirteen times longer than an incandescent bulb and uses 75 percent less electricity to produce the same light. Thus, the light output from a 25-watt CFL equals that from a 100-watt incandescent bulb (the incandescent bulb actually produces more heat than light). CFL bulbs cost more to buy but provide major savings in the long term. Steal a page from Marriott, which saved millions by switching to CFLs—replace your most-used light bulbs with CFLs. Ikea and Home Depot sell a broad selection of CFLs at low prices. Or buy them online. Many of the sites in the **Home** section sell them. Or go to:

www.nolico.com/saveenergy

Meat

(*See also* Farming *and* Food)

www.iatp.org/enviroag/
Download a fact sheet at the bottom of the page called "The Cost of Cheap Food." It shows the health, environmental, and social costs of inexpensive foods.

www.newdream.org/food/beefcost.html
An article about the hidden health and environmental costs of beef production.

www.prwatch.org/books/madcow.html
Mad cow disease has surfaced in the United States? Download the book *Mad Cow USA* free and find out more.

www.themeatrix.com
The Meatrix is a short animated film about the meat industry, with close similarities to a certain hit movie. Watch it, then go to the **Eat Well**

Guide and make healthier choices by buying organic or grass-fed meat from local farmers.

Meetings and Gatherings

www.bluegreenmeetings.org

BlueGreen Meetings offers ideas to hosts, planners, and suppliers who want their gatherings to be environmentally responsible.

Mushrooms

www.fungi.com

Fungi are fundamental participants in the restoration, replenishment, and healing of ecosystems. This fascinating site has much information: about our absolute dependence on fungi; how oyster mushrooms break down toxic oil pollutants in soil, producing a crop of nutritious mushrooms and healthy soil; and the regeneration of soils. There are mushrooms kits for children, and if you want to cultivate mushrooms, this is the site for you.

National Parks

www.npca.org

National Parks Conservation Association.
America's National Parks are national treasures
that perpetually need protection. Check out
Code Red to see if your favorite park is among
the most polluted.

News

Keep abreast of the news. Subscribe to online
newsletters—save money, paper, and energy while
investigating ideas and resources to help you make
informed choices. Many of your favorite magazines, newspapers, and nonprofit organizations
offer this benefit.

www.ENN.com

Environmental News Network. Stay current on
environmental issues with their free daily bulletins.

www.EnvironmentalHealthNews.org

Published daily by Environmental Health Sciences, an organization that aims to help the public understand the science behind environmental exposures and human health.

www.gristmagazine.com

Grist promises its readers "gloom and doom with a sense of humor."

www.motherearthnews.com

Full of valuable advice, this relaxed, friendly site is like sitting around the table with the family talking about the garden and other projects.

www.naturalhome.com

A magazine full of information about how to make your home green.

www.nrdc.org/thisgreenlife

The National Resources Defense Council's monthly newsletter.

www.oriononline.org

A bi-monthly forum on how we can live sustainably on this planet.

www.seventhgeneration.com

Sign up for a free monthly copy of *The Non-Toxic Times*.

http://thenewenvironmentalist.com
Click on **Calculators** to see how simple choices can reduce your impact on the environment.

Nuclear

∽www.kiddofspeed.com∽

The moving photo journal by a young Russian motorcyclist, Elena, who keeps returning alone to the town of Chernobyl after it was rendered uninhabitable by the explosion of its nuclear reactor on April 26, 1986. This site can crash if too many people access it at the same time, but keep on trying. It's really worth it.

www.wagingpeace.org

The advisory board of the Nuclear Age Peace Foundation includes Harrison Ford, Michael Douglas, Helen Caldicott, Daniel Ellsberg, the Dalai Lama, and Archbishop Desmond Tutu. Its mission is to abolish nuclear weapons worldwide, and to use peace as a means of creating a safer world for us, our children, and our children's children. Click on **Issues** to learn about the dangers of nuclear energy and nuclear wastes.

www.kiddofspeed.com

The daughter of a Russian nuclear physicist, Elena is passionate about motorcycles—she rides a Kawasaki ZZR-1100. She was a schoolgirl in 1986 when the reactor of the nuclear power plant at Chernobyl exploded in the early hours of April 26, creating one of the most toxic places on Earth and spreading radiation across Europe for thousands of miles. It may be nine hundred years before anyone can live safely in Chernobyl and the surrounding region again. Through the influence of her father, Elena obtained a pass to travel on her motorcycle into the silent, empty world of Chernobyl. Her photo journal is extraordinary in its simplicity as she observes the devastating effects of the explosion. Forty-eight thousand people had to abandon absolutely everything, even the clothes they stood up in, and walk away from their lives, never to return. Elena's need to record this human tragedy—and make it available for us to see—forces us to recognize the danger of living with nuclear power.

Oceans
(*See also* Seafood)

Overfishing at sea, coastal overdevelopment, and increasing pollution from cities and agriculture are causing the collapse of ocean ecosystems.

www.montereybayaquarium.org
An excellent site with information on ocean conservation.

www.oceanconservancy.org
The Ocean Conservancy works to protect ocean ecosystems and to conserve the abundance and diversity of marine life.

**www.pewoceans.org/
oceans/oceans_pollution.asp**
A review of major threats to the health of the oceans. Pew science reports are known for the high quality of their information.

Office

Because most of us spend so much time at the office, we should take as much care in making that environment healthy as we do with our homes.

www.cleanair-coolplanet.org/solutions
Workplace Greening has many ideas and useful links for those interested in "greening" their offices.

www.dolphinblue.com
and
www.treeco.com
Both of these sites offer environmentally responsible office supplies.

Paper

Paper manufacturing is the fourth most energy-intensive industry and one of the most polluting (but see Södra under **Business** for a different story). Each ton of recycled paper saves 17 mature trees, 3.3 cubic yards of landfill space, 7,100 gallons of fresh water, and 4,100 kilowatt hours of energy. You can recycle household paper and buy recycled paper products including paper towels, toilet paper, gift wrap, envelopes, greeting cards, and stationery. Write to the publishers of your favorite magazines and catalogs and ask them to print their publications on recycled paper.

www.greenbiz.com
For all home office paper products.

www.greenlinepaper.com
Specializes in chlorine-free, recycled, and tree-free papers. They also recycle their packaging and never use those environmentally unfriendly but ubiquitous Styrofoam packing peanuts.

**www.newscientist.com/
news/news.jsp?id=ns99994451**

This article in *New Scientist* discusses the ultimate in paper recycling—erasable ink.

www.rethinkpaper.org

According to the 1998 *North American Pulp and Paper Factbook*, the pulp and paper industry is the largest single industrial wood consumer in the United States and the world. The *Factbook* projects alarming shortages of wood fiber by 2010. ReThink Paper is devoted to studying this issue and encouraging the use of tree-free papers. Find out where you can buy tree-free paper in your state, and learn techniques to lower paper use in your home and office.

Pesticides and Toxins
(*See also* Health *and* Vegetables)

www.ewg.org/reports/mothersmilk/es.php

This report from the Environmental Working Group shows that the concentration of fire retardant chemicals is seventy-five times higher in the breast milk of American mothers than in that of their European counterparts.

http://extoxnet.orst.edu
Created by a group of chemists and toxicologists, this site provides objective, science-based information about toxins that can be understood by all of us.

www.nrdc.org/reference/topics/toxic.asp
For links to sites offering information on toxins.

www.panna.org
Pesticide Action Network North America is part of an international network offering pesticide alternatives that are ecologically sound and socially just.

Plastic and Alternatives

A petroleum-based plastic bag can take centuries to decompose in a landfill. A plastic bag made from corn looks and feels identical but can biodegrade in your compost within a month. At the opening of the World War II Memorial in Washington, D.C., everyone drank lemonade out of plastic cups made from corn. At the 2002 Winter Olympics, Coca-Cola served drinks in similar cups. Rather than ending up in landfills, all those throw-away cups could be composted. The production of corn-based plastics uses up to 50 percent less fossil fuel and emits fewer greenhouse gases than the production of petroleum-based plastics. Biodegradable plastics made from corn are a great example of closed-loop manufacturing. More and more items that traditionally have been made from petroleum-based plastics are now being made with biodegradable plastics based on corn, wheat, peas, and sugarcane. As consumers we must seek out these products and start rewarding their manufacturers by buying them.

www.cargilldow.com

Producers of plastic food-packaging products made entirely from corn. Taiwan has just banned petroleum-based shopping bags and tableware and is replacing them with these biodegradable plastics. The company is also experimenting with other uses for these new plastics. Learn here about the manufacturing process and about how biodegradable plastics benefit farmers, you, the food you eat, and the rest of life on Earth.

www.checnet.org/healthehouse/ education/articles-detail.asp?MainID=26

Why it's a bad idea to microwave food in plastic, plus a list of simple ways to prepare and store foods without using plastics.

www.earthshell.com

Earth Shell's hinged lid container, made from 100 percent compostable plastic, received Green Seal's first certification for rigid food packaging (see **www.greenseal.org** under **Home**). It is economically competitive with plastic and paper alternatives. Plates, bowls, and takeout containers are available, and you can also check out the performance of this company's stock.

www.greenhome.com/ products/kitchen/food_storage

Here you can buy biodegradable "plastic" storage bags made from plants. They contain no petroleum-based plastics. I buy bags from this site and use them for storing food. They are excellent.

www.mindfully.org/Plastic/plastic.htm

In-depth information about how harmful petroleum-based plastics may be to living organisms. Start with **Get Plastic Out of Your Diet**, and then read **Plastics: An Important Part of Your Healthy Diet—Think of Them as the Sixth Basic Food Group**.

www.simplybiodegradable.com

Biodegradable plates, bowls, utensils, and food containers made from corn and sugarcane. Everything you want for the picnic basket and the barbecue. Beautiful serving plates made from tropical leaves.

www.simplybiodegradable.com

For nearly twenty years **Brad Price** studied and worked in the environmental arena writing impact statements on wildlife, fish, and plants, doing water quality surveys, and working in Oregon in a solid waste program. In 2002, while visiting China, he connected with some manufacturers of biodegradable utensils and dishware and immediately started **Simply Biodegradable** to market those products. He believes that these alternatives to petroleum-based plastics are vital for our health and the health of the Earth.

Pollinators

The services of bees, butterflies, birds, bats, flies, and moths are absolutely critical for the pollination of 90 percent of all flowering plants and one-third of all domesticated food plants, yet some of our current agricultural and gardening practices are killing them by the billions. For a better understanding of this problem, explore the following sites and their valuable links.

www.lubee.org/who-whyconserve.aspx
Explains the critical role that fruit bats play in human welfare.

www.nappc.org
North American Pollinator Protection Campaign.

Questions

Good questions are as important as good answers. Here's a question: how can we make environmentally important actions attractive and engaging to the general public? Please send your answers to:

ideas@oceanalliance.org

Reduce-Reuse-Recycle

(*See also* Batteries, Cell Phones, Trash, *and* Waste)

www.earth911.org

Enter your ZIP code and discover your local recycling resources. Get information on fire prevention, wet cleaning (a healthier alternative to dry cleaning), beach water quality, and water conservation.

www.epa.gov/epaoswer/ non-hw/muncpl/reduce.htm

Explains the principles of the three Rs.

www.freecycle.org

This site facilitates the free exchange of stuff that some people no longer need and that others are desperate for. If your town is not yet involved in the program, you can find out how to start a local group. This is a great way for a community to get and give things, eliminate waste, save money, and conserve landfill space. Membership is free.

www.FundingFactory.com

Recycle your empty inkjet and laser cartridges

and other things while helping schools and non-profit organizations.

www.nrc-recycle.org

The National Recycling Coalition's 4,500 members include people from business, all levels of government, recycling companies, and environmental groups who work together to improve all aspects of the recycling business. A very informative site.

www.nrc-recycle.org/resources/ electronics/index.htm

Recovery, reuse, and recycling of electronic equipment. Offers advice and free technical workshops about the design, manufacture, and purchase of environmentally responsible electronic equipment.

www.realmoney.org/articles/recycling.htm

A site that helps you make some money while getting rid of the clutter in your basement.

www.sharetechnology.org

This site connects those who want to discard a computer with those who need one.

Note for the family couch potato: each recycled beer can saves enough electricity to run a television set for three hours.

Republican Party

Turning environmental protection into a political football is one of the most short-sighted political mistakes ever made. If ever there should be a bipartisan issue, a healthy environment is it. Following Teddy Roosevelt's lead, many other Republican presidents have acted to protect the environment. Eisenhower established part of the Arctic National Wildlife Refuge. Coolidge and Hoover set aside such treasured places as the Grand Canyon, White Sands, Arches, Glacier Bay, and Death Valley, and Nixon established the framework for today's national environmental laws.

www.repamerica.org

A site for Republicans who want to restore the Grand Old Party's traditional support of the environment.

Seafood

(See also Fish)

Seventy-five percent of the world's fisheries are either exploited to their maximum capacity or overexploited. In the last fifty years, industrial fishing practices have wiped out 90 percent of tuna, halibut, swordfish, and grouper. Some fisheries could disappear before today's five-year-olds have learned to drive. Fish farming is not the whole answer, since fish farming practices can produce unhealthy fish and threaten wild populations of the same species. Use the following sites to find out about the problems of overfishing and the dilemma of eating farmed fish.

www.ecofish.com

EcoFish is a small company in Portsmouth, New Hampshire, that promotes ecologically responsible consumption of seafood. This site is for purveyors of fish as well as consumers. Check out **Species** and **Links** at the bottom of the page.

www.ecofish.com

Lisa and Henry Lovejoy worked in the conventional seafood industry for fifteen years. During that time they often visited huge international fish markets like those in Tokyo and Paris. They constantly saw many threatened species being sold, and they came to realize that the seafood industry was not addressing the growing problems of over-fishing and the subsequent destruction of fisheries worldwide. So in 1999 they launched **EcoFish** and started to sell only sustainably produced seafood. It became the first seafood company in the United States that the Marine Stewardship Council certified. Today **EcoFish** products are sold in restaurants and in over one thousand natural food stores nationwide. At the end of 2004, they plan to launch their Foodservice Program, which will introduce sustainably produced fish in popular chain restaurants such as Applebee's and T.G.I. Friday's. Henry says, "The tide is turning. The natural products industry is the fastest growing sector of the retail market in the United States—25 percent per year for the last five years. This is wonderful news for the planet. It shows that you can make money while being environmentally friendly."

www.ewg.org/reports/
BrainFood/sidebar.html

The Environmental Working Group recommends which fish pregnant women should avoid eating because of mercury contamination and suggests healthier choices. Mercury is toxic to the developing fetal brain, and exposure in the womb can cause mental development delays and life-long learning deficiencies.

www.freerangegraphics.com/
flash/flash3.html

Check out the delightful film on Chilean Sea Bass. Then send it to your local restaurant. I've shown it to dozens of friends.

www.lobsters.org

The Lobster Conservancy is dedicated to ensuring a continued supply of lobsters and the success of the lobster industry. Both are threatened by pollution and over-harvesting. You can adopt a lobster here.

www.msc.org

The Marine Stewardship Council promotes environmentally healthy seafood choices through the use of its MSC label—the only international standard that assures consumers that the fish they are buying are sustainably produced. Recipes, facts, and where to find stores that sell fish with the MSC label.

www.seafoodchoices.com

The Seafood Choices Alliance provides ocean conservation information to fishermen, marketers of seafood, and restauranteurs to help them make sustainable choices.

Farmed Salmon

These three sites address the negative sides of salmon farming:

**www.ecotrust.org/publications/
farmed_salmon_steak.html**

www.ewg.org/reports/farmedPCBs/es.php

**www.davidsuzuki.org/Oceans/
Fish_Farming/Salmon**

Shopping Bags

Although they are handy, single-use plastic shopping bags waste resources and cause big problems. Every year, the United States consumes an estimated 12 million barrels of oil manufacturing plastic bags that end up in landfills after one use, where they can take one thousand years to decompose. If left to blow in the wind, they become deadly food for seabirds, sea turtles, and whales, or they accumulate as tiny, long-lived fragments—a serious and growing hazard to marine life. When a marine animal dies and decays, the plastic bag survives to be eaten by another animal and to kill it. Take multi-use shopping bags with you next time you go to the supermarket. Always have one in the trunk of the car. You can find multi-use bags on the following sites:

www.ecobags.com
and
www.reusablebags.com

Or be creative and make your own.

Simple Steps

SIMPLE THINGS ANYONE CAN DO:

⚘ Don't leave the faucet running when shaving, brushing teeth, or hand-washing dishes. ⚘ Turn off lights you're not using. ⚘ Turn off computers and monitors when you leave for more than an hour. ⚘ Unplug electrical chargers when not in use. ⚘ Replace your most-used incandescent bulbs with compact fluorescents. ⚘ Walk, cycle, bus, or carpool instead of driving. ⚘ Use pump sprays, not aerosols. ⚜ Use cloth napkins instead of paper. ⚜ Use a clothesline rather than a dryer whenever possible. ⚜ Recycle. ⚜ Compost. ⚜ "Use it up, wear it out, make it do, or do without."

Teachers

Educators are on the front line of the battle to engage and excite young minds about the overwhelming complexity of the environmental problems we face. Here is some ammunition for that fight.

www.cln.org/themes/recycle.html
Ideas for how to teach recycling to school children.

http://earthballoon.com/resource.htm
An extensive list of links for teaching about the environment.

http://pathfinderscience.net
Great ideas for science projects.

www.pbs.org/odyssey/class/index.html
Use lessons on whales to get children interested in the oceans. Check out **Class from the Sea**.

Rocky Mountain Institute for Kids offers excellent classroom resource materials on energy and water.

Thermostats

By turning the thermostat down three degrees in the winter and up three degrees in the summer you'll save yourself more than $50 and the world nearly 1,100 pounds of carbon dioxide emissions every year.

Transportation

www.amtrak.com

Remember passenger trains? They're still one of the nicest, most relaxing ways to travel, and they burn much less fuel per passenger than cars do.

www.auto-free.org

Auto-Free New York is a movement aimed at bringing better-functioning mass transit to the core of the most densely populated city in the United States: New York City. It also attempts to reduce car use and create auto-free spaces in the core.

www.eere.energy.gov/cleancities

A comprehensive site with excellent connections to information about alternative transportation. Click on **Alternative Fuels and Vehicles** for information on biodiesel, electricity, ethanol, hydrogen, natural gas, and propane fuels. Click on **Advanced Technology Vehicles** for information about hybrid electric, electric, and fuel cell vehicles.

www.egovehicles.com

An energy-efficient electric bike with style.

www.electric-scooter-world.com

Electric scooter product reviews.

www.onwardvia.org

Onward Via promotes sustainable, affordable, and safe transportation for Boston. Perhaps this site will inspire you to start a similar effort in your community.

www.planettran.com

Decrease the impact of your air travel on the environment by letting the Boston-based company PlanetTran drive you to Logan Airport in a Toyota Prius. America's first, exclusively hybrid gas/electric car service.

www.planettran.com

On New Year's Day 2003, Yale graduate **Seth Riney** was reading a book about environmental entrepreneurship when he began thinking about taxis and limousines. He wondered why most public vehicles on city streets were big, inefficient gas-guzzlers. The idea of **PlanetTran** came from those musings. He decided to start the first urban livery service in Boston, using only hybrid electric/gas vehicles as the foundation of a sustainable urban transportation system. Hybrid vehicles get sixty miles to the gallon in the city, which should be a big economic incentive for taxi companies to follow Seth's example.

www.sustainable.doe.gov

Site for the Smart Communities Network of the U.S. Department of Energy. Click on **Transportation**.

Trash

(*See also* Compost, Reduce-Reuse-Recycle, Worms, *and* Waste)

Trash is one of our biggest products. Some towns in Canada and the United States are beginning to collect organic waste separately from trash and turn it into compost. Get your town to do the same to improve soil and relieve pressure on the garbage dump.

www.americanrecycler.com/ 0504municipal.shtml
An article about successful municipal composting in the United States.

www.coverall.net/waste/fundy.html
Recycling at its best—the method by which municipal organic waste is collected, processed, and sold as organic material for much-needed topsoil.

www.greenbiz.com/news/ news_third.cfm?NewsID=26909
The California supermarket chain Vons composts all trims and culls from their stores. In ten years they have turned 377,826 tons of "trash" into compost, which they have given to schools. This is the closed-loop system at work.

Travel

The choice of how and where you travel can have a big effect on the places and people you visit. More and more people are becoming interested in eco-tourism—a way of traveling that protects the environment while improving the well-being of local peoples and making them stakeholders in maintaining their ecosystems.

bluewaternetwork.org/ campaign_ss_cruises.shtml

Cruise ships are major ocean polluters. Learn about this problem and what the Bluewater Network is doing to try to solve it.

www.ecotourism.org

The International Ecotourism Society offers resources for the traveler and for travel businesses. This is a good place to start.

www.greenchoices.com/id42.htm

More choices for interesting eco-holidays.

www.greenhotels.com

Green Hotels benefits those of us who want hotels to reduce solid wastes and save water and energy. It also benefits people in the hotel business. Members receive *Guidelines and Ideas*—110 pages of environmentally friendly ways to save money while saving the Earth. Travelers can find addresses here for green hotels throughout the United States, Canada, South America, the Caribbean, Europe, and Africa, as well as green travel hints that include what to do before you leave home.

www.greenseal.org/greeninglodge.htm

Find a list of lodgings approved by Green Seal. The Green Seal is given to products and services that conserve habitats, produce little or no toxic pollution and waste, and limit their release of gases that contribute to global warming. The organization has no interest in the products or services it endorses.

http://h.webring.com/hub?ring=ecotouring

There is somewhere for everyone in this world-wide list of ecotourism sites.

www.outwardbound.com

Outward Bound offers over 750 safe, adventure-based wilderness courses serving adults, teens, and youth. Courses range from rock climbing to sea kayaking, from dogsledding to sailing, and more. Participants learn self-reliance, compassion, and a sense of responsibility toward both the team and the environment.

www.responsibletravel.com

This site puts you in contact with over 170 leading tourism businesses worldwide. They offer a wide choice of eco-friendly holidays ranging from a farm in New Zealand to a chance to volunteer in the Arctic, studying climate change.

Eco-resorts

www.bayoffires.com.au
Two ecological adventures in faraway Tasmania.

www.polepole.com
Pole Pole is a resort in the Mafia Island Marine Park, a protected ecosystem in Tanzania.

www.shompole.com
A luxury safari camp in Kenya at the edge of the Great Rift Valley, run in partnership with the local Masai people. Funds from this camp go toward schools, clinics, and the maintenance of the prolific wildlife in the area that surrounds the camp.

www.tiamoresorts.com/world2.html
Billed as the "Caribbean's most environmentally sensitive hotel operation," this Bahamian resort is working hard to set new standards in eco-sensitive resort development.

Trees

Trees are essential to our well-being and to the well-being of life on Earth. Their beauty is a blessing, but they are being destroyed by the pressure of human needs. Here are some of the many sites that explore this problem.

www.arborday.org

The National Arbor Day Foundation. Find out about trees, use the online tree identification guide, learn about the immense problems impacting rainforests, get free trees, buy trees for yourself, and give them as gifts.

www.forests.org

The Forest Conservation Portal is a gateway to over three thousand sites addressing forest ecology issues, deforestation and its consequences, the vital importance of the rainforest, and the absolute necessity to harvest all forests sustainably.

⌇www.treesftf.org⌇

Trees for the Future is a great example of what one person's determination to change the world can do. David Deppner's grassroots organization plants trees worldwide (nearly SIX million in 2003) to counteract the effects of global warming. It also links young people here in America with children in the developing world to increase global awareness. Check out the **Trees for Travel™** program and how to make your gas-guzzler a **Global Cooling Vehicle™**.

www.treesftf.org

David and Grace Deppner are taking on the environmental threat of global warming from their home. What used to be the front bedroom is now the office for **Trees for the Future**, a nonprofit they started in 1988. In the Philippines, David had seen squatters by the thousands driven into Manila because the denuded land could no longer support them. In South America, he had seen how deforested agricultural land was unable to hold any moisture from abundant rainfall because of lack of trees. He had seen African women walking miles to find firewood for cooking. This former Peace Corps volunteer— together with his team of like-minded souls— started planting fast-growing trees in the developing world to help restore the ecology and offset the effects of carbon dioxide emissions, a primary cause of global warming. They have also helped more than 6,500 villages in Asia, Africa, and the Americas to develop their economy with environmentally beneficial projects. They planted nearly six million trees in 2003. David likes to say that he's lighting a candle instead of cursing the darkness. As a fellow churchgoer said of him, "Dave's taking on global warming single-handedly. If more people would do what he's doing, the world would change."

Universe

See the glory of the universe within which Earth is but a speck.

http://antwrp.gsfc.nasa.gov/apod
Each day receive a different, stunning image of the universe, along with a professional astronomer's explanation of what you're seeing.

www.darksky.org
Light pollution keeps us from seeing the stars. The International Dark Sky Association encourages the use of outdoor lights that shine only downward so we can reclaim the night sky.

www.nineplanets.org
Go on a multimedia tour of the solar system.

Vegetables

(*See also* Food)

If each American ate two fewer meat dishes each week for a year, the grain that otherwise would have been fed to feedlot animals would be enough to feed 225 million more people for that whole year.

www.foodnews.org
For a downloadable guide to the vegetables that are most and least contaminated with pesticides.

Vinegar

You can use white vinegar as a cleaner, to help with the laundry, and even to get bugs off plants. The following sites will help you find out more.

**www.newhomemaker.com/
cleanorg/vinegar.html**

www.superbherbs.net/sec6.htm
Click on **Vinegar the Miracle Cleaner.**

www.versatilevinegar.org

Volunteering

⟨⟩ **www.crossculturalsolutions.org** ⟨⟩
Cross-Cultural Solutions takes volunteers to South America, India, Russia, Thailand, and Africa, and works to build understanding and peace. CNN called this "an amazingly humane and caring organization."

www.earthwatch.org
Take part in scientific field research worldwide with the Earth Institute. Restore trees to sacred groves in India, monitor hawksbill turtles on the Great Barrier Reef, assess the nutritional status of endangered rhinos, or map water resources to avoid potential conflicts.

www.easi.org
The Environmental Alliance for Senior Involvement utilizes the knowledge and skills of older people in efforts to protect their communities and the environment for the well-being of future generations.

www.ecovolunteer.org
Work with Przewalski's horses in Mongolia or wolves and Karakachan shepherd dogs in the mountains of Bulgaria. Watch belugas mating and giving birth during the white nights near the

www.crossculturalsolutions.org

In 1994, **Steve Rosenthal** bought a one-way ticket to Nepal. He had been working as an engineer for AT&T, but decided that since he had grown up in America, it was time to see the world and gain a deeper understanding of other cultures. From Nepal, he traveled for a year through India, Thailand, Indonesia, Uganda, Egypt, Kenya, Jordan, and Israel. Upon returning home, he realized that the most important part of his trip had been a week he spent in Kenya, helping a friend in the Peace Corps build a medical clinic in a small village. During that week he ceased to be a tourist and became a member of the village, part of a team building an essential service for that village. He began wondering whether he could find a way to give others a similar experience. He went back to India and started connecting with grassroots organizations to find out if they needed volunteers to live and work in their communities for a year. The result was the establishment of **Cross-Cultural Solutions** in 1995. It now operates 18 programs in 11 countries, has 250 staff members in 15 offices worldwide, and has placed more than 7,000 volunteers all over the world.

Solovetski Islands in Russia, or help in a new study to find out how orangutans self-medicate in northern Sumatra. These are a few of the many exciting choices offered to you by Ecovolunteer.

www.greenvol.com
Green Volunteers is a worldwide guide to volunteer work in nature conservation.

www.gvi.co.uk
Global Vision International uses volunteers from all over the world to work on aid-related projects. Enjoy a wildlife conservation expedition to the Amazon rainforest, take part in a marine life census in the Seychelles, or become part of the South African National Parks Internship Program. Minimum age is eighteen.

www.thesca.org
The Student Conservation Association. Become an intern and have an adventure!

Vote
(*See also* Democracy)

All members of a healthy democracy should vote. It is one of our most important civic duties, because by voting we can influence the environmental policies of our government. Many of the sites in this book give you the opportunity to register to vote if you haven't already done so. You must believe that your vote counts, and know that it only will count if you exercise your democratic right to vote.

www.DeclareYourself.com

Register to vote here, find out where your polling place is, or get an absentee ballot form if you need one.

www.doubleyourvote.com

Register a friend.

www.fec.gov/votregis/vr.htm

Download a voter registration form.

www.rockthevote.com

Rock the Vote encourages young people to register to vote, and then gives them the tools they need to become effective members of the democracy and influence the issues that matter most to them. Comedians, musicians, athletes, and actors all contribute to this youth-driven site. Check out the **Public Service Announcements** (PSAs).

Waste

Waste is one of our major problems. Today's delight becomes tomorrow's trash, and the Earth is dying under the pressure. It is becoming more and more difficult to cope with the amount of waste we produce. Because one species' waste is another's resource, the natural world has no such thing as true waste. Like it or not, we are part of the natural world, and therefore must obey natural laws—laws that are far more powerful than any that governments can pass. That means that we too must turn all our wastes into resources for the rest of life. This is what the Zero Waste movement is all about. Using nature's closed-loop system as its model, it is building a revolution for the twenty-first century. The following sites are full of information about this new way of living that is happening all over the world.

www.beyondwaste.com

A California company that deconstructs old buildings and resells the salvaged materials for building new ones. Better than just bringing in the bulldozers! It also trains people in the skills necessary for this growing industry.

www.ecocycle.org

A grand success story about a group of people in Colorado who believed in conserving natural resources and made Boulder one of the first twenty cities in the United States to offer curbside recycling. They believe that instead of managing wastes we should all work toward managing resources to eliminate wastes.

www.grrn.org

Grassroots Recycling Network. Click on **Zero Waste** to see how you can start a zero waste project in your community.

www.grrn.org/zerowaste/articles/ biocycle_zw_commentary.html

Zero Waste defined.

www.secondharvest.org

Second Harvest's mission is to end hunger in America. It encourages growers, wholesalers, restauranteurs, and caterers to donate unused food to food banks rather than dump it. The uneaten food from conferences, memorial dinners, wedding parties, supermarket shelves, and restaurants should not be thrown away to waste. It could all go to feed the millions who are hungry in this country.

www.state.ia.us/dnr/energy/main/programs/methane/index.html

Find out how farmers in Iowa are using methane recovery as a renewable energy technology that helps livestock operations, wastewater treatment facilities, and landfills turn waste into assets.

www.zerowaste.org

Zero Waste Alliance. Click on **The Case for Zero Waste** and see why zero waste is essential to our survival.

Wastes, Hazardous

www.earth911.org

Click on **Household Hazardous Waste** for a helpful directory for how and where to dispose of your household hazardous wastes.

http://outreach.missouri.edu/owm/hhw.htm

How to dispose of household hazardous wastes. Guide sheets with a ton of information. An essential site.

Water

(See also Composting Toilets *and* Educating Yourself)

Less than one percent of the Earth's water is fresh water that can be used for drinking, irrigation, and industry. By 2025, the United Nations expects that 3.5 billion people will experience water shortages. As aquifers dry up, rivers dwindle, and droughts spread, access to fresh water—something we in America take so much for granted—will become a serious problem. Learn about the problem and what you can do.

www.awwa.org/community/links.cfm

The American Waterworks Association provides a wealth of information about water-related topics, including conservation, research, landscaping, access to healthy drinking water, better building design, and information on getting rebates when you save water.

www.earthday.net/goals/waterfacts.stm

Learn about why there is a water crisis, the seriousness of the crisis, and what we can do to start remedying it.

www.livingmachines.com

Living Machines, Inc., builds solar-powered wastewater systems that mimic nature by using microorganisms, plants, fish, and small invertebrates to process sewage and wastewater. Its end product is reusable water that can be used to water parks, gardens, and golf courses; help to cool industrial plants; flush toilets; and aid in construction work, fire-fighting, and washing your car. This is another good example of a closed-loop system.

See a Living System at work in the Discovery Center in Kansas City, Missouri; at the National Audubon Society's Corkscrew Swamp Sanctuary near Naples, Florida; and at Ethel M Chocolates in Las Vegas, Nevada (At **www.ethelm.com**, click on **The Living Machine** at the bottom of the page), where the system treats 32,000 gallons of highly concentrated industrial wastewater a day and reuses it to irrigate their famous cactus garden.

At present the biggest of these extraordinary systems is in Wyong, Australia, where the Master Foods Company uses it to process 200,000 gallons of wastewater per day.

www.newint.org/issue354/facts.htm
The basics of the water crisis laid out clearly.

www.rmi.org/sitepages/pid123.php
Efficient ways to use water in your household.

Weddings

www.marriedforgood.com
Share the joy of your wedding day by donating the extra food, giving the flowers to the local hospital, and the like. For your honeymoon, see Travel.

www.twistedlimbpaper.com
Beautiful invitations, handmade from 100 percent
recycled paper.

Whales

www.oceanalliance.org
Click on **Voyage of the Odyssey** and join my husband's research vessel *ODYSSEY* in its five-year
worldwide ocean pollution study, which is being
done with the help of sperm whales.

www.wdcs.org
The Whale and Dolphin Conservation Society
maintains a worldwide database on where to go
whale watching.

Worms
(*See also* Coffee, Compost, Gardens, *and* Trash)

www.happydranch.com
Remove your food waste from the trash and put
your own worm farm to work converting it into
nutrient-rich, 100 percent organic fertilizer for
your potted plants and garden. A project for the
kids.

X Chromosome

That which makes a mother. The mother of all is
Nature. Her cradle is the Earth.

www.oneearth.org
Click on **Communications**, then **Campaigns**, and
view the films made for each year. Start with
1995 to see a film called *Mother*.

Young People
(*See also* Vote)

**www.bygpub.com/books/
tg2rw/volunteer.htm**

Twenty ways for teenagers to volunteer. Get out from under that cloud of boredom. Become involved in something that can be fun. You'll feel good about yourself as you make new friends and help others, and you'll increase your sense of self-respect while discovering skills you didn't know you had.

www.changetheworldkids.com

A group of twenty-one young people in my hometown of Woodstock, Vermont, who started giving their services free to the community: building clotheslines, helping seniors, repairing substandard housing. One of their biggest projects is in the Costa Rican rainforest. They have planted hundreds of trees to help save critical migratory corridor habitats for songbirds, have started a tree nursery, and are working with local coffee farmers to support their growing of fair-trade coffee.

www.ecomall.com/biz/kidslinks.htm
A catalog that describes how the world works.

ibuydifferent.org
A site for young people created by the World Wildlife Fund and the Center for a New American Dream.

www.idealist.org/kt/youthorgs.html
Environmental organizations started by young people.

www.kids4hydrogen.com
Kids 4 Hydrogen was started by fifteen-year-old Jaclyn D'Arcy to educate children and adults about the hydrogen revolution, and why it must become America's future energy source.

www.kids4hydrogen.com/articlesk4h.htm
An inspirational article by Jaclyn D'Arcy.

www.kidsface.org
Kids for a Clean Environment was started in Nashville in 1989 by nine-year-old Melissa Poe.

www.kids4hydrogen.com

Fifteen-year-old **Jaclyn D'Arcy** is counting the days until she gets her driver's license. She is determined that her first car will be hydrogen-powered. To that end she has been interning with an auto mechanic to learn about the workings of the internal combustion engine, and taking classes in the techniques of converting such an engine to hydrogen. By the time she turns sixteen, in February 2005, she aims to be the proud owner of a car powered by hydrogen. She hopes that because hydrogen will someday be cheaper than petroleum and healthier for the environment, many young Americans will follow her example. That's why she started **Kids 4 Hydrogen**. She is concerned that current leaders are making energy decisions that will negatively affect future generations, and she is working hard to give young people a forum to demand cleaner, more efficient, and more sustainable fuel.

www.yesworld.org

YES! Youth for Environmental Sanity educates, inspires, and empowers young people to live their ideals on a daily basis.

www.kidsface.org

In 1989, after watching *Highway to Heaven*, an environmental program on TV, nine-year-old **Melissa Poe** decided that she did not want to grow up in a polluted world. Believing that children can make a difference she started **Kids for a Clean Environment** with six friends at her school in Nashville, Tennessee. One of the first things she did was to write a letter to President George H. Bush asking him to do something about pollution. In April 1990, that letter appeared on billboards across America. She spoke at the Earth Summit at Rio in 1992. Her group has distributed and planted over one million trees. Their latest project is 2001: Earth Odyssey, which focuses on children's health, animal survival, and the loss of land and wildlife habitat. Melissa is now Executive Director of **Kids for a Clean Environment**, and is busy fundraising and dreaming up new projects. The little club of six has grown to more than 300,000 members worldwide.

www.youthnoise.com/page.php?page_id=229
A toolkit for young volunteers describing ways in which you can stop being part of the problem and become part of the solution.

Zero Population Growth

Overpopulation is the root cause of every environmental problem. The key to survival on our planet is population control. Support organizations that work humanely to bring net human population growth to zero.

http://opr.princeton.edu/popclock
A world population clock. Watching it count is a sobering experience.

www.populationaction.org/issues/index.htm
Population Action International lays out the problems that runaway population growth causes, including its impact on humanity's hopes for peace.

www.populationconnection.org
A national, grassroots, educational organization specializing in problems concerned with population growth.

Lisa Harrow was born in New Zealand and went to London to study at the Royal Academy of Dramatic Art, after which she joined the Royal Shakespeare Company. She has appeared on Broadway as Vivian Bearing in *Wit* and in numerous plays and films, including *All Creatures Great and Small*. Lisa is married to Dr. Roger Payne and they live in Woodstock, Vermont. Together they have written and produced a performance piece called *Lessons From Copernicus*. The play offers vivid evidence of the thousands of practical, affordable steps we can all take to preserve our fragile planet and make the world a better place. *What Can I Do?* was originally created as a kind of citizen guide to action for the play and was given away to the audience at the end of each performance.

Dr. Roger Payne has studied the behavior of whales since 1967 and is the founder and president of Ocean Alliance. He is best known as codiscoverer of humpback whale songs, and for his theory that fin and blue whale sounds can be heard across oceans. He directs long-term research projects on the songs of humpback whales and on the behavior of Argentine right whales. His many publications include the book *Among Whales* (1995) and three recordings, *Songs of the Humpback Whale* (1970—record holder as best-selling natural history recording), *Deep Voices* (1975), and *Whales Alive* (1989). He is a writer and presenter for television documentaries, and cowriter and codirector of the IMAX film *Whales*.

Get Inspired!

Great books to help you change the world

SUSTAINABLE LIVING has many facets. Chelsea Green's celebration of the sustainable has led us to publish trendsetting books about innovative building techniques, regenerative forestry, organic gardening and agriculture, solar electricity and renewable energy, local and bioregional democracy, and whole foods and Slow food.

For more information about Chelsea Green, visit our Web site at www.chelseagreen.com, where you will find more than 200 books on the politics and practice of sustainable living.

paperback | $10.00

paperback | $10.00

paperback | $16.95

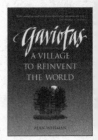

paperback | $16.95

CHELSEA GREEN is committed to being a sustainable business enterprise as well as a publisher of books on the politics and practice of sustainability. This means reducing natural resource and energy use to the maximum extent possible. We print our books and catalogs on chlorine-free recycled paper, using soy-based inks, whenever possible. *What Can I Do?* was printed on Legacy Trade Book Natural, a 100 percent post-consumer waste recycled, old growth forest-free paper supplied by Webcom.

CHELSEA GREEN PUBLISHING | the politics and practice of sustainable living
www.chelseagreen.com